Socialize Like a
Homeschooler

Socialize Like a Homeschooler

A Humorous Handbook for Homeschoolers

Jennifer Cabrera

Hifalutin Homeschooler

Socialize Like a Homeschooler

©2018 Jennifer L. Cabrera.
All Rights Reserved.

Cover and illustrations by
Jennifer Cabrera

For my D boys.

If you only remember one
thing I have taught you,
remember this:
If it were easy, everyone
would do it.

Contents

"We wagered a second income on the notion that we could educate our children more effectively than the public-school system. We wagered the need to fit into the world's expectations on the belief that our children should look to us for social and moral guidance. We wagered the ease and comfort of kid-free time on the belief that kids need family more than peers, love more than affirmation, and encouragement more than conformity."

-Hifalutin Homeschooler

100 Hilarious Homeschool Manners

Manners for the Homeschooled Kid Out in Public During School Hours

1. When someone asks why you are not at school today, do not roll your eyes and say...*Here we go again!*

2. Also, do not simply say... *I don't go to school.*

3. Resist the urge to ask... *Well, why aren't you at work?*

4. For the love of second breakfast, comb your hair before you leave the house. Let's break the mold already.

5. Want to save yourself from further annoying questions?
    Just make up a name for your homeschool and give it to strangers who ask where you go to school. When they say they've never heard of it, tell them it is too elite for most people.

6. Do not tell people you go to Hogwarts Academy. The Proper Name is Hogwarts School of Witchcraft and Wizardry.

And where exactly is this school of yours?

Platform nine and three quarters.

HifalutinHomeschooler.com

7. If a stranger asks if you like your teacher this year, do not say... *No, she sleeps with the principal.*

8. If you decide to tell a stranger you homeschool, do not look weepy to attract pity. You will be alone with your mother shortly.

9. When asked what grade you are in, do not say... *What subject?*

10. Rehearse what grade you are in before leaving the house. There is no such thing as 14th grade. That is just your age.

11. Knowing you homeschool, if someone asks the ridiculous question, *Do you like your teacher?,* do not roll your eyes and look annoyed.

12. The proper response to the question *Do you like your teacher?* is *No, I love her.* Remember whose team you are on.

HifalutinHomeschooler.com

13. At the doctor's office, do not laugh or scoff at the nurse when she asks if you need a note to return to school.

14. Do not make the nurse write you a doctor's note only to then turn and hand it to your mom and ask to be excused in sheer mockery.

15. Give the docents at the museums time to finish asking their questions before you answer them.

16.

Clean up after yourself throughout the day. Your mom already does the work of 7-10 well paid employees, except without the pay part.

17. If a stranger asks how you will make friends if you are not in school, just ask... *Well, you aren't in school, so how do you make friends?*

18. When someone asks that worn out question about socialization, just tell them... *we're nonbelievers*. Their bumfuzzled horror will give you time to get away.

19. When you are driving by a school on your day off, do not make weird faces at the kids on the playground or yell out the window...*See ya, suckers!*

20. Correcting the grammar
    of strangers or adults is
    strictly forbidden.

21. Do not audibly refer to the school bus as the "indoctrination bus."

22. You may **not** wear your school uniform when outside of the house. Pajamas at the museum and grocery store give all homeschoolers a bad reputation.

23. By all means, wear your Batman costume everywhere.

Are you sure you want to wear that again?

No one would recognize me in plain clothes, Mom.

HifalutinHomeschooler.com

24. When you see a yellow bus, do not yell...
Don't let them take me!

Homeschool Manners When with Public Schoolers

1. When you are with public-schooled kids that tease you about being homeschooled, do **not** say... *Oh, you go to public school. I'm sorry your mama doesn't really love you.*

2. When another kid asks if you get tired of being at home every day, do not in turn ask... *Do you get tired of sitting at a desk in the same classroom with the same people day after day?* You already know the answer is yes. Do not rub it in.

3. Do not refer to public school as "kid prison" and the kids who attend as "inmates."

4. Do not follow up #3 by asking... *What cell block, um, I mean what grade are you in?*

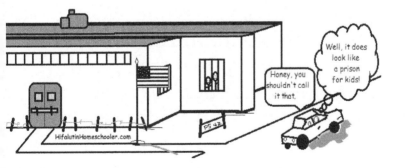

5. Stop droning on about your latest projects and ask other kids about their interests and hobbies. Though you usually rule your school, the world does not actually revolve around you.

6. Bragging about sleeping late, short school hours, no standardized tests, exciting field trips, and learning at your own pace is fun to do. But it makes you a snot too. Do **not** do it.

7. Okay, you can do #6 occasionally, but not too often. We do not want word to get out and our parks and museums to start getting crowded on weekdays too.

8. Never assume that all kids know and love *Blimey Cow*. Do not bother explaining it either. They probably will not get it.

9. Do not instigate an academic decathlon with your cousins in the living room at the family Christmas party. You might not win.

10. Try not to laugh when your public-school friends do the *Whip*, *Nae Nae*, or *Dab*. They know not what they look like.

11. If you want to have friends, do not continuously correct other kids. It is great that you know Abraham Lincoln was a Republican, pasta originated in China not Italy, and black holes are not actually *holes*. But, no one likes a know-it-all.

12. Do not make private jokes in Latin.

Homeschool Manners for Moms

1. You do not have to tell everyone you meet that you homeschool. It just leads to nosy questions and unwanted opinions. Then suddenly, you find yourself arguing with the gas station attendant about your child's college prospects.

2. If someone is concerned that you homeschool and points out that you are not a certified teacher, look completely shocked like you had no idea.
Then whisper...
Shhh, don't tell my kids!

3. Politely answer questions from the curious. Some people really do not understand how you homeschool.

4. Never say anything negative about homeschooling in front of a skeptical audience.

HifalutinHomeschooler.com

5.

Do not throat punch anyone who rudely disagrees with your choice to homeschool. Jesus loves them too, dang it.

6. When other moms say they could never homeschool, do **NOT** agree with them. Or do, and watch their faces.

7. Some moms will often tell you they cannot homeschool in hopes you will argue with them. Refrain. Simply say... *Well, not everyone should homeschool.* It lets you off the hook. They can wrestle their own demons.

8. The question, *Is that even legal?* is an accurate indicator that the person speaking is against homeschooling. Abort the situation asap.

9. Be bold and ask for the teacher's discount at all the stores. But do not fly over the counter when they tell you *no*. Go home and print a teacher ID. It is like a fake ID for teens, but with better perks.

Hifalutin School of Awesomeness

TEACHER:
Hifalutin Homeschool Mom

GRADE:
All the Grades and then some

School Address:
Home, duh.

Expires: Never

THIS IS MY TEACHER I.D.

HifalutinHomeschooler.com

10. When someone says you must be really patient, immediately scream at your kids... *Hurry up! We don't have time for this nonsense!*

11. When someone asks how long you plan on homeschooling, it is probably best not to ask them how long they plan on wearing their hair like that.

12. If they ask about socialization (and they will) tell them... *Oh, we don't believe in that. We're Solitairists.*

13. Or say this: *I want them to be weird.*

14. Or maybe try this:

They are my kids. I'll screw them up if I want to!

15. Let friends and family know that calling during the hours you are homeschooling is only excusable with a note from their doctor.

16. If they call anyway and ask if you are busy, resist the urge to hang up. Just continue teaching right into their ear.

17. The next time a telemarketer calls and interrupts school, put them on speaker phone. Then let your kids practice their new logic skills to pick apart whatever scam they are peddling.

18. Teach your kids to answer the phone in several different languages. Telemarketers will actually hang-up on you.

19. In case the doorbell rings unexpectedly, have a bra stashed in a handy location.

20. Tell the UPS guy to please not ring the doorbell every time he stops by, unless he is looking to be the next career day speaker.

HifalutinHomeschooler.com

21. Do not correct other people's kids at the library. Even though you refer to the place as your family's second home, it is a public facility.

22. Do not complain about your child's teacher at co-op for not teaching to your standard. She is probably working for free and you could always teach it your own way at home.

23. If you catch an adult conducting a round of jeopardy on your kid to assess their academic knowledge, allow your kid to question the adult right back. Taking turns is good socialization.

24. When someone says they could never homeschool their kids, but then asks if you would do it for them, just laugh. They are joking, right? If they say *No, really. Will you homeschool my kids too?* ...RUN!

Homeschool Manners for Dads

1. Teach whatever you can, whenever you can.
   Do not limit yourself to garage and outdoor lessons. You can conjugate a verb as well as the rest of us.

2. Those daily maintenance jobs you do around the house make for one heck of a life-skills course. Let the girl-child enroll too.

3. *Sounds of Bodily functions 101* is an outside study course and can *only* be practiced when alone or in the car with dad.

4. If you say you are going to teach something, then actually follow through and teach it. No points for good intentions.

5. Brag about your wife as often as you can to whomever will listen.

6. Let your wife hear you brag about her. Remember she will **not** get a bonus check or employee of the month plaque no matter how incredible she performs.

7. Yes, you too can get a library card.

8. Be ready to cook or pick up pizza on a moment's notice.

9. Be able to recognize the times she is going to need you to pick up pizza. She may not realize it herself.

10. *Ooh and aah* over all the paintings, drawings, crafts, and unidentifiable items you are proudly presented with when you get home from work.

11. Never sleep during family read-aloud time. There might be a quiz. "Resting your eyes" is not an acceptable excuse.

12. It is especially important that you do not fall asleep if you are the one reading.

13. When the kids ask you a question, *Go ask mom…* is not the answer.

14. *I don't know, let's Google it…* is acceptable.

15. Listen, smile, comment, make coffee and enjoy looking at homeschool curriculum on-line. This is the equivalent of bringing flowers and chocolate home.

16. No getting irritated and annoyed with the kids if you have only been home for five minutes.

17. Set a timer on your phone when you are on the toilet. You get thirty minutes, tops.

Homeschool Manners Between Homeschoolers

1. Other homeschoolers should understand the struggles of other homeschoolers. Let others vent their frustrations as you do yours; in a safe space, no judgements.

2.

Deschooling, unschooling, classical schooling, eclectic schooling, or whatever-you-call-it schooling are all the different labels we assign to our individual purpose and collective exhaustion. Respect each other.

3. If another homeschool mom asks for advice, tread lightly and within the confines of the request.

4. Remember, your method
    is not the only method of
    homeschooling. Play
    nicely.

5. No matter how innocent
    your intentions, do not
    point out what you think
    another homeschool
    mom is doing wrong.
    Just let that train wreck
    and fix itself.

6. To co-op or not to co-op? Remember, moms are expected to participate.

7. Many awesome homeschool moms have left their co-op or never joined one in the first place. Just bow out gracefully.

8. Never claim to use the best curriculum. "The Best Curriculum" is such a relative term that even Einstein's head would spin.

9. It is okay to brag about your kid's academic achievement (in moderation) around other homeschool moms. Just be mindful of those struggling with learning disabilities, and celebrate their achievements as well.

10. It is okay to get annoyed with moms who brag about their kid's achievements. Just be mindful that they may not know your kid is struggling, and they are not the cause of the struggle.

11. Help that new homeschool mom out by airing some of your dirty laundry; like the time you tried to give a spelling test in the dentist's waiting room.

12. Learning Latin is quite commendable, but does not make you an elite homeschooler. Do not snub those who choose to learn one of the other foreign languages of the living.

13. Be kind to the mom who decides to quit homeschooling. Her shoes do not fit your feet.

14. Some of us homeschool parents let our kids eat the red dye #40. We do not feel guilty, so don't try and make us. Trust that we are laden with other guilts.

15. Some homeschoolers really do make and eat their own kale chips. Do not make fun of them. They may live longer than the rest of us.

Manners for Others When Socializing with Homeschoolers

1. When you meet a homeschooler, count to three before saying or asking whatever just popped into your head.

2. Do not assume all our kid's behaviors are a result of homeschooling, unless they are being awesome. Then yes, this is because they are homeschooled.

3. We are not actively recruiting new members. So please, do not feel the need to explain why you do not homeschool when you meet us. We really do not have the time or energy to care.

4. Every concern you have about our choice to homeschool has crossed our minds at least seven-thousand times. You need not bring it up every time we meet. No really. Just stop.

Oh, you mean I'm not a certified teacher? Thanks for letting me know before I really made a mess of things!

HifalutinHomeschooler.com

5.

It is true. There are homeschoolers who cannot read and are socially awkward.
But there are thousands more just as illiterate and tragically weird, and they are sitting in public schools across the country. Stop the finger pointing.

6. Homeschoolers are not "normal." This is one of our proudest qualities. But be careful what you say. The movement is growing, and you do not want to eat your words someday. You know, in case you decide to give it a shot!

Hifalutin Observations & Insights

- I have all but scientifically proven that a child will not sharpen their pencil until such time it will cause the loudest, most annoying ruckus guaranteeing a sibling will be shot into orbit or will break his/her own pencil in half and slip into insanity.

- Co-op is all at once fun and a waste of time. In a moment of weakness, we joined a co-op. You either love it, hate it, or put up with it. You will not understand this until you have been there thinking to yourself, "This is alright, but what more productive thing could we be doing right now?"

- You will find that as homeschool parents, there are plenty of things other than money to argue about.

- Curriculum shopping is way underrated. Internet scrolling through all the educational possibilities is intoxicating. Reading the reviews, comparing the samples...Ahhh!

- A trip to the mailbox can save your soul between math lessons and grammar. The mailbox is one of my favorite hangouts.

- Just because they offer a class somewhere does not mean you cannot teach it better at home. You might be that mom at co-op smiling and helping-out, but all the while thinking, *I could make this so much more interesting,* and wishing you never signed up in the first place.

- There are homeschoolers who never seem to be at home. They are in every club in the county, three different co-ops, six sports, church groups, the peace corps, and take a vacation every thirty minutes. Just open a *Where's Waldo* book and you are guaranteed to find them on every page.

- Remember, no matter how difficult the subject, grade level, age, or school year, this too shall pass. And then there is calculus.

- Even homeschool moms form cliques. With all the different reasons and ways to homeschool we are probably more equipped to discriminate against one another than our public-school counterparts.

- Never try to talk anyone
  into homeschooling. It is
  like urging a friend to
  marry someone that you
  do not even know. You
  do not have to live with
  them, so stay out of it.
  Likewise, never argue
  with someone adamantly
  against homeschooling.
  Both could end in hurt
  feelings, or a homicide.

Most Popular
~~And Lame~~ Excuses NOT to Homeschool

1. "You must be really patient. I get too frustrated with my kids."

<u>Hifalutin Thoughts:</u>

If I were patient I would have given up homeschooling years ago. We would never get anything done. We would probably be covered in mold or turned to stone still waiting for one of my twins to finish his writing journal from our first Monday as homeschoolers.

It is because I am short on patience that we get things done. I like things done right, yesterday. I do not sleep well when things are not done.

When one of my boys is typing a final draft for a writing assignment, I must sit on my hands not to tear the keyboard from the desk and type the dang paper already!

2."I can't homeschool. My kids don't listen to me."

Hifalutin Thoughts:

Every time I hear this one I want to respond with *I'm sorry, what did you say?* then walk away.

Seriously, all children are born deaf. And the condition only temporarily subsides when you are on an important private phone call locked in the bathroom whispering with the water running in the sink. Then, your kids are guaranteed to hear every word and repeat them to all who will listen to what they have learned while eaves dropping.

Because of this phenomenon, I am tossing around a new curriculum idea where you teach history like an eavesdropping gossip chain. And here is how it works:

The teacher will hide on the toilet and whisper conspiratorially...

"You know that uppity girl named Joan who thinks she's so special? Well, she said she can, like, lead an army for her friend the king. (pause) I don't know, girl. I heard she may have a crush on him. (pause) Mmmhmm. And get this: she says God told her to, and everyone was like, No way! And she was like, Way. And you know what? She did it! She fought like a beast, all hair pulling, swords, and crazy cat claws and stuff! That king should have named a holiday after her. But, I hear he just wasn't that into her, because someone called her a witch and he didn't even take up for her. And now, I smell smoke! Girl, for real."

I am still working out the syllabus and other details, but you get the idea.

3. "I could never homeschool (*insert difficult child's name here*). We argue about everything."

Hifalutin Thoughts:
Well, yes. And?

Some kids are visual learners. Others are kinesthetic or auditory. Two of mine are argumentative. Duh, ever heard of debate?

My children and I argue about everything from the true reason for commas to which way is up if the earth is round. A child that will not argue is either asleep or cannot form an original thought because they have been taught to follow without question.

Many of our disagreements still end with me saying, "Because I said so!" But when my kid can form a mature argument, I'm proud they have at least learned to think and build up ammo for a stance.

Of course, I'm opposition and

moderator. So, speak your mind, honey child, but unless Wikipedia can back you up, I still win.

4. "You are much braver than me. I just can't be with my kids that much."

<u>Hifalutin Thoughts:</u>
Why? You don't like them? Will you turn into a pumpkin? Is there a restraining order?

This excuse always perplexes me. I am often left wondering if being separated from her kids is to keep mom safe from her kids, or her kids safe from her. I think this lame excuse is really code for, "I'd rather be doing something easier."

Real Expectations and Tips for New Homeschoolers

- Get a real dictionary for your classroom, not the ones from the $1 bins. Apparently the 10,000 words they left out did not qualify for the discount.

- Your child that hated math in school will most likely still hate math.

- You may look over the teacher's manual and realize **you** still hate math.

- The crystals will never look like they do on the box, or may never grow at all.

- Real money is better than the math manipulatives. Teach them to identify it, count it, make change with it. Then bribe them to finish their work with it.

- As a free thinker yourself, you will want your children to think critically. They will. And they will question the necessity of everything you ask them to do.

- That expensive, award winning curriculum will inevitably suck. You will determine this only after you have torn out pages or your children have written in the book.

- You will start to worry about socialization when your kids do not know how to do the *Stinky Leg* (or whatever is the new dance craze) at the team party.

- You will quickly discover it is best to write your lesson plans in pencil. Very lightly.

- Just go to the movies. CPS is not camped out behind the neighbor's begonias. If public schools can take all day field trips to six flags and call it educational, you can go see the new *Diary of a Wimpy Kid* movie and call it journalism.

- Painting Xs on the driveway for PE is kind of a ridiculous idea that will not wash off.

- You may need to do a tick check after your family nature walks.

- You cannot make grammar *funner*. Punctuation bingo is not as exciting as it sounds.

- If you find your kind of homeschool mom-pal, realize it fast enough to keep from sticking your foot in your mouth and commenting on how many kids are following her around.

- Grilled free-range chicken breast atop organic greens is not a practical lunch option. Microwave taquitos are a God send.

- One day your child will know more about the topic you are trying to teach than you do. And you will suddenly feel completely inadequate all over again.

- Only when out in public will you notice your child is wearing his/her shirt on backwards, unmatched socks, is a month overdue for a haircut, and basically looks like the poster child for homeschooling.

- The library will be able to host elaborate parties with the late fees it collects solely from your family. And you will never even read half the books you check out.

- Your child will reminisce about everything fun (and fantasy) about public school and how they miss having friends all in front of your biggest homeschool critic.

- No one agrees completely with how you are homeschooling. Be the bold captain of your own ship. But try not to throw anyone overboard.

- There is no title or trophy for being the best homeschool mom. Do not let this stop you from pretending there is and trying to earn it. Working on an acceptance speech is probably too much though.

   However, I would like to thank all those moms who made it a fun race.

10 Things
I Hate About
Homeschooling

1. Being the cafeteria lady.

Which is kind of ironic because my kids say their favorite thing about homeschooling is the food. But three meals a day plus snacks seven days a week gets old real fast. And I am not even talking about the money it takes to feed three growing athletic boys with a hollow leg each.

I hate grocery shopping. And yes, the bill could rival the national debt by the time I have gotten them all to the chest hair phase. But even if your kid goes to school you have to buy or pack the lunch, right?

What I hate is the actual prep and clean-up that comes not once, not twice, but thrice a day. I have got minds to mold and rulers to crack! This feeding gig gets in the way.

We stock up on breakfast and lunch foods they can easily nuke for themselves in the microwave. Figure in condiments for those frozen burgers, tacos, sandwiches, and explosive leftovers, and then I get to play drill sergeant to get it all cleaned up in time to finish history before we leave for swim practice.

And it is always fun to teach cooking class at dinner time to impatient, not so careful starving kids. Except when it's not. Then you just want a glass of wine and half the loaf of French bread you are buttering while you peruse Facebook and stir the powdered cheese into the macaroni.

2. Being the heavy.

All those cute jokes about making out with the principal and getting away with it are hilarious. But around here, being principal is on par with being the Queen of England. A respected position with little discernible immediate authority or job requirements (except to pretend to be ready to inflict severe consequences from an undisclosed location. I.e. at work).

Consequences cannot wait till after evening rush hour if we are doing math right now and my child says he just "*ain't* doing math" and hides under his desk.

There is no teacher the children and I can bond in contempt of for assigning the work they must complete before computer time. Yep, that teacher is me, Cruela D'Mom. I am the enforcer of all things deemed unnecessary and inhumane such as grammar, flash cards, reading time, capitalizing every sentence, acceptable handwriting, throwing away goldfish wrappers, getting dressed for practice, and flushing the toilet *every* time they use it.

3. Reading about how awesome the curriculum is that I am **NOT** using.

If you have never shopped for curriculum piece by piece, then you have probably never covered your eyes and played "any-many-miney-mo" with the computer screen.

We homeschool eclectically. This is code for *I'm a control freak who can't make up her mind*. There are pros and cons to classical education, literature vs. textbook reading, Saxon vs. Singapore, religious vs. secular, cursive vs. print, crunchy vs. smooth, peddling oils vs. peddling make-up etc. Why should we have to choose just one?

Every summer I lay awake for hours for nights on end reading reviews, watching ads, and researching to find the golden ticket medley of courses to guarantee future college scholarships. And when I finally lay the money on the table and commit to the dealer, I cringe with doubt as the tabloids of success roll in for the programs I turned down. Did I win or lose this hand?

4. Feeling that every decision I make as cruise director could sink their ships in the future.

Homeschool moms worry about everything imaginable. Should we school year-round? How many extracurricular activities are enough? Does each child need to play a musical instrument and a sport? *Should they* have a fun hobby on top of all the academics?

If we decided to skip the review on adjectives, did we write off a chance at the *New York Times Best Seller List* someday? Should they go to a regular high school? Will they fit in or stand out? What if they don't stand out? What if I forget to teach them something essential and they go to college not knowing how to use a combination lock? Should I go buy three combination locks?

What if they are too gentlemanly and mistaken as sexist by today's young woman? If we do not visit Disney

World often enough, will they ever learn to wait in line like good citizens?

5. Needing to be left alone while simultaneously feeling lonely.

It is possible to be having your ear talked off by multiple people at once and feel like you are on a deserted island and no one cares if you get hit on the head with another Minecraft coconut. Hiding on the toilet with a book is almost as good as a trip to the grocery store for nothing in particular, just gloriously without the kids.

If I am having a particularly hard day of whiny children and goals not met, but rather hurled out the window, who would care to hear about it? Even the dog runs and hides on those days.

Homeschool moms are strong and independent and must keep up appearances all the time, so that those special friends or relatives cannot jump at the chance to tell them they could *see this coming*, and that it is *okay they failed*.

Am I supposed to have time for real, 3D, non-internet based friends? And if I find some time, do I have the energy left to be a good friend?

6. The pay sucks.

And so do the taxes. We knew this going in, but did not fully appreciate it until really looking at what we spend on educating our boys at home to the best of our abilities. The amount of money we are paying to help educate everyone else's kids far surpasses what we can spend on our own. There are no tax breaks for homeschool families.

It is sad that I can write off a set of mugs we donated to charity during our recent move, but I cannot write off six hundred dollars-worth of textbooks and supplies, which are used by someone working for free to educate kids not utilizing public services, and therefore freeing-up tax dollars for other children's public education.

7. The excitement I expect is rarely met.

Let me just say that doing all of elementary school for the second time has been a blast. And to think, I once despised being forced to learn multiplication and write how-to essays for someone to comically follow verbatim.

How fun is this? Ha-ha! What was I thinking? Now I'm all *Woohoo! Let's do this!*

At the start of each new school year I am usually jumping around on too much coffee and enthusiasm and waiting for the boys to explode with joy as I outline such things as how they are going to each research and then present one of the three branches of government.

Wuh whaah. Charlie Brown enters with, "Oh, I got the legislative branch, they don't do anything." And thus, the wind is knocked out of my sails.

This does not happen every time though. I did orchestrate the burning of London to a wild applause. It is understandable for the age difference that we get excited about different things. I am looking at life from the opposite direction, and with experienced perspective.

I want so bad for them to see with my eyes. And I will not quit trying. Like a cheerleader trying to rouse the crowd while the players cry on the bench, 4th quarter, 36-0.

8. Being called a stay-at-home-mom.

Did you just refer to me as a stay-at-home-mom (SAHM)? I am the *Matriarchal Academic Ninja!* That makes me the M-A-N!

It really should not bother me, and most of the time it does not. I know people who admittedly go to work to get out of the task of SAHM. It is not for the weak. But homeschool moms are the SAHM 10.0, the souped-up version with antivirus software. We work even with a tissue stuffed up both nostrils and a low-grade fever.

9. Telemarketers, wrong numbers...

...right numbers at the wrong time, UPS, Fed-Ex., meter readers, mailmen, handymen, solicitors, door-to-door salesmen, Jehovah's Witnesses or anyone with a pamphlet I did not ask to read.
People who say they will be here sometime between 8am-5pm.
Do-gooders who kidnap my **not** lost dog from our street and call me to come get him across town.
Folks I love dearly and anyone else that shows up when I am minutes away from finishing an important lesson, and who thus make me envision stabbing them with my red grading pen.

10. Not knowing if anything I am doing is working until they are gainfully employed, independent, upstanding men, husbands and fathers.

Obviously, some of what I am doing is working. My kids can perform a multitude of tasks on or above grade level. But the deep seeded reason for homeschooling is to instill stalwart moral character and create productive members of society.

Whether they become fry cooks or surgeons, engineers or repairmen, plumbers or senators, I want them to be genuine, strong, Godly men. All we can do is point them in the right direction, arm them with knowledge and morals, and pray for the strength to see them through. And then we must let go and realize they will have to do the rest on their own. And remember to breathe.

About the Author

Jennifer Cabrera is the witty writer at HifalutinHomeschooler.com. Her articles and memes offer homeschool parents comradery and comedic relief from the highs and lows of homeschooling. Jennifer is married and lives in Texas where she homeschools her three exceptional boys. She began homeschooling after butting heads with a public-school system that values conformity over individual potential. Her boys are in it for the food.

Hifalutin Homeschooler

"The opposite of common is remarkable, and cafeteria food sucks."

Web:
www.HifalutinHomeschooler.com

Email:
HifalutinHomeschooler@gmail.com

Facebook:
www.facebook.com/hifalutinhomeschooler/

Made in the USA
Monee, IL
18 December 2022